MYSTERIES OF

-BIRTH-
-SEXES & LOVE-
-DEATH-

Translation of
Integral 3 Chapters from
"Clefs de l'Orient" 1877

Alexandre Saint-Yves d'Alveydre

ALEXANDRE
SAINT-YVES D'ALVEYDRE

Initiation to the Mysteries of BIRTH SEXES & LOVE DEATH

Main 3 Chapters from the original French work "Clefs de l'Orient" published in 1877.

Translation from French and Commentaries by
SIMHA SERAYA *and* ALBERT HALDANE

MANAKAEL
MASTERWORKS

For information contact Publishing Management:
MANAKAEL MASTERWORKS INC
E-mail: *archangel7997@gmail.com*

Visionary Metaphysical.
Categories: Keywords
Philosophy, Religion, Spirituality, Mythology, History.
Secrets in Early Christianism
Birth
Sexes
Death
Soul Immortality
High Mysteries

First Edition

ISBN 13: 978-0-9837102-8-8

Printed in the United States of America

Cover design by BUZBOOKS.com

DEDICATION

To Alexandre Saint-Yves d'Alveydre,
savant, thinker and visionary.
1842-1909 Paris, France

REMARKS:
All foot notes and commentaries are written by the
translators Simha Seraya and Albert Haldane.

According to the customs of his time the author
SAINT-YVES D'ALVEYDRE is inserting his
commentaries in the main body of the work.

FOREWORD

Saint-Yves d'Alveydre published these "MYSTERIES" in 1877 in a book -titled "Clefs de l'Orient"- primarily destined to the official diplomats and statesmen engaged into international–negotiations, at a time when the European nations were on the brink of a military clash with Turkey, then the leader of Islam.

The preface itself (not presented in this book) issues this urgent warning: *"The imminence of a clash between Turkey and one of the great powers of Christendom will lead to and is already leading to a religious awakening of all Islam. This awakening will eventually lead to military storms with serious consequences for the Christians and the Mohammedans…"*

Fully aware of the imminence of that impending catastrophic "clash of civilizations", Saint-Yves warns that usual recourse to refurbished ordinary thinking will not suffice this time.

Today's readers facing obstacles or oppositions of their own, are here urgently invited, as an indispensable step, to explore and seek answers to 3 Fundamental Mysteries:

BIRTH
SEXES AND LOVE
DEATH.

It is Saint-Yves' anticipation that true solutions to apparently unsolvable problems, will be found *only* when one accepts to explore the primal sources and real origins of the predicaments.

And as those Fundamental Questions concern all sentient humankind, it is *each and every human being* who is concerned by the Answers provided in those 3 chapters titled "Mysteries".

Albert Haldane Simha Seraya

January 2021

TABLE OF CONTENTS

Is there something as solemn as Death?
Yes, BIRTH!

Life is the smile of Nature; *Birth* is the kiss Nature gives to the human soul.

Respect to the Woman: the real presence of Nature is in her.

Ionah,[1] the plastic virtue of Nature, lives in her and is delighted to do so.

Rouah,[2] Spirit and Love, are descending from heaven to rest and play in her heart; the great secret of creation smiles upon her through the new child, when a

---

[1] IO-NAH=personification of Divine Supra-Nature.

[2] According to Moses' teaching, before Birth the soul is a ROUACH: Whirlwind (ROU) of the Spirit of Brotherhood-Sisterhood (ACH). After Death souls transmute into NESHAMAH: Essences (NE) of Heavens (SHAMAH).

1

soul having descended into the woman looks at her through a newborn's eyes.

Immortal after Death, the Soul is certainly immortal before Birth. Through the feminine medium, the ancestors return into the generative cycles within human societies.

The immortal ancestors are called to reintegrate social life, in accordance with the Mysteries of the Holy Spirit and with the Mysteries of the Supreme Father.

Said in a secular manner, the immortal ancestors descend at the intended time, and destined place, embodying their spirit within a newborn child subject to physical death.

During this process, which begins with an inflorescence of immortality, the soul, according to its rank in the psychurgical hierarchies, leaves one of its cosmogonic residences, and begins its descent.

Invisible, but sensitive to loving hearts, the descending soul seeks the woman it has to haunt, and during 9 lunar revolutions, through the mother's blood

2

and the mother's soul, it entangles its sidereal fluxes with the growing terrestrial body; then, at birth, the infant, at the very moment of its first breath, will engulf the descending soul[1].

This name soul, "âme" in French, is magnificently in conformity with the celestial Verb.

It is the very root of love, "amour" in French.

What is the soul?

Let's decipher, with the appropriate keys, the Hebrew text of *Sepher Behreshith*, at the Chapters expounding the Cosmogonic Principles, and, God willing, the Divine Science of the Egyptian Sanctuaries will answer us with the words of Moses, telling us what *Isha* is, that is: the volitive faculty of *Ish*.

---

[1] The Jewish Tradition teaches that, after the birth of the infant, the *Rouach* (spirit descended within the infant) and the *Nefesha* (organic spirit of the mother) continue their entanglement for 40 days. During that period the mother keeps the newborn nearby, both being inseparable. All domestic duties are therefore delegated to other family members or helpers.

Moses, venerated ancestor, has revealed the first level of the hidden meanings; but no more than he, do I wish to unveil the second meaning, except later, in the second chapter, after having elucidated the Mystery of the Sexes and the Mystery of the Name of Jehovah.

Here is everything I can say for the moment: *immortal principle of Existence, radiant cause through the visible body and the invisible body, the soul IS*.

Theurgy allows to find and attain the divinity of the soul; Psychurgy, which is the transcendental Science and Art of loving, wishing and willing, can *prove experimentally the existence of the soul*.

Even at the level of physiology, the soul is no less than the foundational Force that animates and moves, attracts or repels, elects or eliminates.

Therefore, Birth is a solemn sacred event; Love and Genders are sacred phenomena; and nothing is trivial in Nature, any more than in the Divine realm.

Birth is the corporealization of souls.

4

Be aware, you preexist your Birth, and you will survive your Death. Therefore, in the name of Moses, in the name of Jesus and Muhammad, stand up! And listen!

To know is to reminisce.

Let us then remember together, O immortal Souls, who, residing within the terrestrial species, aspire to the heavenly reign of humankind, and crave for living in the divine plane.

The Mysteries of the Holy Spirit reveal the knowledge of the Integral Science, the Grand Art, the perfect Love for Life!

Upon earth those Mysteries are felt in the daily magnificent sunrises, in the radiant eyes of fiancés and newlyweds, in the smile and joyful tears of motherhood.

Gently bend over this crib, at once zenith of social life and crypt of the cosmogonic soul.

In the heart of this infant pulsates the Holy Spirit, enigmatic presence of the Mother Spirit, the celestial Spouse of the celestial Father.

Be aware, this newborn child is an ancestor, a celestial soul terrestrially embodied, an Immortality that comes to mortify itself, to purify itself in pain, to perfect itself in an ordeal, to pursue, where and how it is necessary, either an atonement or an experiential growth, being always the continuation of a creative mission, initiated since centuries and renewed again and again.

Therefore, to the wise, the inequality of living conditions, even in an advanced social state, is but only what it ought to be: defined by the standard of equity by which are ranked the degrees of transcendent personal awareness, and outlined by the necessary requisites for the soul to exert its good will within the social sphere corresponding to that of their projected destiny!

This is why access to true explicit knowledge, by an Initiation modulated according to Genders and personal degree of Consciousness, is commanded by Providence, so that the individuals cease to curse their lot which, most often, is but the upshot of their own will, thoughts and behaviors.

But, I know, rational science alone cannot enlighten your soul.

Therefore, I intend to borrow from the Grand Art a psychurgical secret, and thanks to it, slowly, the ancient poets and prophets of the sublime Promise will eventually attract your soul, immersing it into the flow of the ethereal Light of the Holy Spirit.

So, newly born in the world of effigies and painful tribulations, this soul, screams!

Its original elemental milieu was the celestial fluid, the inner light of the universe, the ethereal spirit, the inner primordial side of the cosmogonic substance.

Now it finds itself upside down, outside, in the middle of a night.

It cannot anymore see its own celestial body, for it has vanished.

This soul has now lost its real science, its real consciousness, its real life. Its inherent intelligence is closing, its direct clairvoyance no longer perceives, its celestial intelligence no longer discerns, its psychurgic transcendental receptivity is ubiquitously overwhelmed.

Between the soul and the Universe rises a terrible obstacle, something obscure and impeding, convoluted, obtuse, acrid and searing, a strange compound that gurgles and swarms; folded on itself and surrounding the soul, a veil skillfully and artistically knit, of which all entwined animated textures, precise reflections of the Universe, all mirroring, in a specific conjunction, the faculties of the Soul.

Faculties and universe reflections entwine themselves while embracing the Soul, infusing the tortuous forms of the organs and viscera: the soul is now embodied!

If the body screams, it is because the Soul is suffering.

The Soul attempts to flee; but it falls back under the first maternal kiss, soft irradiation reminiscent of the Universe living Light, Ionah, the Celestial Substance.

At times the soul feels it is dying, or almost dead. Like in a dream, the Soul reminisces about the immensity of that arcane Light when, naked, it was immerged in the resplendent whirlpools, peaks, ethereal valleys of a beloved star devoid of material atmosphere, free from any physical attraction.

As this soul was living within a world of pure essences, aromas and fragrances of Life, she was hearing the ascending and descending Harmonies, Inner Melodies of Times and Spaces, of Beings and Things; a world whence, quivering, it emerged, responding to the intimate voice of other souls, beloved companions, inviting it to contemplate *Shamaim*, the *Aether*, the azure Sea of Heaven, the celestial islands, the sidereal fleets, their movements directed by their inspiring Genii-Angels and animating Puissances.

Like a star's reflection on undulating water, a memory of the majestic cosmic reality descends, still pulsating, within that Soul.

The soul still exhales the heavenly ambrosia, quintessence of the Holy Spirit's eternal Mysteries.

And the fragrances of the other World are yet emanating ever slowly out of the balsamic essence which the new mother breathes, inhales and kisses with that unique strange exhilaration incomprehensible to the others.

Do not fly away, sweet reflection of the Magi's Star! Immortal Soul, remember!

Your spirit is still filled with visions of the shining beings, the divine men and women, goddesses and gods, diaphanous glowing forms, archetypes of Beauty, chalices of the Truth, soaring and hovering, intertwining with the magical waves of celestial Love, in the dazzling communions of pure Sapience.

Your remembrance now encompasses the Sacred Processions:

Here come the Occult Verb's Living Poems,

and the Hymns to Creative Thoughts,

the Symphonies of Harmonic Emotions,

followed by the Hierarchical Teachings of the transcendent Psychurgic Circles, the Holy Dazzling of the Initiatic Higher Mysteries,

and then come the Gods, congregated within the Ray of the Supreme God, whose Light is but the shadow, the luminous furrow, the aromatic flight of Genii and Envoys, Perfect Intelligence, Immortal Spirits, victorious and glorified Souls.

O vertiginous horizons!

Here, appears the quadruple lower circle of ascending or descending souls, the fluidic, sparkling ocean, above which blows the breeze of Love; and from this oceanic bottom rise the screams of Birth and Death.

Isn't more coming? ... But what was I going to say?

What is happening? Sing, sing, daughter of the Gods!

Listen!

A great confusion, a giddiness, a sudden elation, sweet and terrible attraction, an incantation of the Stars, a command, a scream echoing from sphere to sphere, poignant adieu to the Higher Life, to the beloved ones, a prayer , solemn funeral rites, a last embrace, a last kiss, a pledge to remember and return, a winged Genie seizing the descending Immortal, leading it towards the chasms.

Now the Immensity above is closing, the Vastness below opens with a crash.

The soul enters the tumultuous Ocean of the Generations, abysses where the Souls attain the peaks or leave the bottom of another star's atmosphere; it is now reaching Earth and its electric battles of passions and instincts... then ... what?

Now appears the orb of the Earth, with its metallic Ocean unfurling its fluxes, revolving its tides.

The descending soul now traverses over whirlwinds of souls that rise or fall, some diaphanous and pure, spiritualized and light, exhorting themselves to sway those souls who resist climbing up the ladder of celestial rays, those who oppose crossing the expanses of Celestial Clouds and fluidic currents, those reluctant to reach the Igneous Citadel of the Higher Fire, the circles of Aether.

Other souls, shadowy and marbled like the skins of wild beasts and reptiles, soiled by vices, darkened by crimes, densified by crude instinct, weighed down by obtuse egoism, powerless to break the aerial Electric Rivers, carried away by Storms and Winds, rolling away from the boat of Isis, diving in the demonic pit of the Abyss, (this vertiginous cone of darkness the Earth drags in the Heavens), those souls, crying in Silence, clinging to the ascending ones, are pulling them down along, in a last attempt to lessen the dreadful weight of their own Fate.

And what now? Remember!

Here appearing in the Atmosphere, the vaporous Clouds, the great Polar Currents, the breaths of the East, the gusts of the West, the aerial Rivers stirring the vaporous clouds, shaking the winding electric fluxes; here is now the lower Ocean of the Air, with its four descending levels,

first the eagles,

then the great migratory birds,

then the larks and the doves.

In this last lower expanse, begins the reign of the Plastic Substance on Earth, with its four Divisions: Mineral, Vegetal, Animal, Hominal, and its seven Vortices of Generative Puissances, with their resulting Specified Creations.

After the dizzying cirques and amphitheaters of the white mountains, after the dazzling fairyland of the Glaciers and the Gorges, now unfold to infinity the soft undulations of green hills, the frothy flow of torrents, the writhing metallic rivers, the oscillating resonant forests, the circular immensity of the verdant landscapes, where grass blades curve and play.

This is the Earth, one of the thousand Citadels of the Kingdom of Man, the immortal and mortal Son of the God of the

Gods, here is Demeter, *Adamah*, the world of the effigies and Physical Realities.

It is Hell or Purgatory or Paradise, depending on the quality of the incarnating Soul, depending on the specific epochal Spirit who reigns in the flesh of already incarnated Souls, and in accordance with Faith, Law, and Mores of the present Social milieu.

Here surge the stone circles of the Metropolises, Cities, Towns and Villages; here resonate the voices of the bronze bells which, from the top of domes and steeples, rhythm and announce all the Births and all the Deaths, over the din of the wide popular life streams.

The incoming Immortal Soul abruptly stops; fastening itself strongly to the brightness of the Stars, it assesses how far in space it has traveled, the distance now separating it from the Heavens:

- ***Have Mercy***! Says the soul imploring its Guide.

-" Be Brave! You pledged it! Up there, the crown of Faith, down there the Tribulations! "

- "Forgive me! Yes, I'm scared! What if, down there, I am unable to gather my memories!"

- "You will do so by gathering Sciences."

- "At least, tell me where am I emerging? In which Social State, Race, Nation, Home?"

Responds the Winged Guide of the Souls:

- "Here the celestial *Genethliac Science* will teach you the weft and warp of your destiny."

- "For a long time?"

- "Until completion!"

- "O my cherished Winged Genie, what are these choirs that are following us?"

- "They are the Ancestors who will continue the procession with you; for, now, I am leaving you and will climb back."

16

- "Already? I feel faint again!"

-"Take Courage, immortal Soul! I will come back for you if you know how to will it."

- "Where am I now? Heaven, Earth, everything has vanished; but an invincible attraction enchains me entirely."

- "Mortal soul, here is your Mother"

"In the name of God, in the name of Nature, in the name of *Iod* [1]and *Hevah*[2], here is your living homeland here below.

"Be united to her by all the magical powers of Life!

"Adieu". Farewell!

Reminiscences.

The incoming soul now remembers its conversations with the hovering maternal soul, their indivisible and mutual entanglement, their mysterious communions fraught with memories and hyper-terrestrial aspirations, their pains and joys,

---

[1] IOD=reflection of the Divine Father's power.
[2] HEVAH=reflection of the Divine Mother's spirit.

17

thrills, ecstasies, silent musique, the slow gyrations of nine lunar months, the incantation of the epigenetic unfolding.

And then …

a crucially terrible suffering, a sulfurous vapor, a ferruginous effluvium rising abruptly from the igneous Caverns of the Earth, swirling, tearing it apart from the maternal soul, nailing the new host onto an inflated void, a warm, moving pulmonary cave ...

a cry in that cave, in that hollow effigy and ... the Memory returns back to its original profundity, re-conjoining with the ontological celestial Principles, source of all Existences.

Here that original Memory and Reminiscence will be re-acquired only through Integral Sciences.

O you men who are shamefully claiming an origin as low as the level of the gorilla, you deserve to remain there!

Stay away from this Heavenly Mystery and let Women invoke and pray. At least they will be able to utter: "Our Father who is in Heaven."

As for you, stand up, Virgins, Wives, Mothers, Grand Mothers, Druidesses of the Tree of Life; stay close to this living Mistletoe, pray the Ancestor of the Ancestors.

And know that, whereas, in the cycle of Generations, the human male Father provides the seed of the effigy, the initial movement of the Species, it is the female Mother who provides substance and specified form; contrary to the souls of the animals that come partially from the Earthly Fire, the Human Soul comes entirely from the Heavens.

Therefore, call a Priest, so that in the name of the Social Organism, the Human Species may salute the Law of the Superior Regnum and the Order of the Divine Kingdom.

What priest, will you say?

The cleric from within your own Faith and your Social Mores:

orthodox pope, priest, pastor, rabbi or mullah.

Make sure this newborn is solemnly welcomed.

> *For, truly, I say to you, BIRTH is as solemn as Death.*

In earliest Christianity

the transcendent foundations of the *separation* of the Sexes and the *unification* of the Sexes through Love were not destined to become common knowledge:

-the spiritual fundamentals concerning the *Sexes*[1] were included only within the Initiation to the "High Mysteries of the Father",

-the spiritual fundamentals concerning *Love* were included only within the

---

[1] Sexes are the manifestation of the Cosmic Principle of polarization, triggering at the same time 2 opposite Forces: separation coexistent with reunion through Love–attraction. Genders are the perceptible manifestation of that Principle on the physical plane of reality.

Initiation to the "High Mysteries of the Holy Spirit[1]".

In the primitive Church, these Mysteries were clearly reserved for Higher Education, an equivalent to authentic Initiation.

Thus, this intellectual and highest level of teaching was well safeguarded; during terrestrial life, access to the Divine Kingdom was open only to the Epopts[2] or the Elects; and, wisely, it was differentiated from the moral or primary teaching common to all.

At the first level of common teaching, the *Baptism* was offering *Purification* to the souls; the second level, represented by the *Eucharist,* defined the ontological values,

---

[1] The Holy Spirit is a term which secretively designates the Mother Spirit also designated "Infinite Spirit".

[2] Epopt (plural epopts) An initiate in the Eleusinian Greek Mysteries; one who has attended the epopteia meaning one instructed in the mysteries of a secret Highest Science.

induced the intelligences to contemplate *Perfection*, and to compenetrate It, at the level of knowledge and the degree of consciousness each student could comprehend, in correspondence with their gender, age, and rank.

The authentic Initiation, giving access to the Mysteries, was open only to the small selection of those who, prepared by the evangelical vulgarization, or catechization under lengthy observation, were deemed predisposed to receive explicit revelations, specific, and conform with the degree they had attained in the hierarchy of sexes, ages, and ontological ranks.

In contrast, for the Catechumens,

the teaching was what it has become today, common to all the faithful indistinctly, uniform and uniformly applied, limited to Catechization and Preaching.

For those non-initiated Catechumens, most numerous necessarily, the Mysteries remained veiled behind the sacraments, truths being comprehensible only through sensory symbols.

"The custom of the Church" says St. Cyril *"is to not reveal to the Gentiles[1] its Mysteries, especially those regarding the Father and the Mother-Holy Spirit."*

"The Church does not even mention this subject to the Catechumens.

"When it does, it is almost always in veiled terms, so that the educated faithful can nonetheless understand, while the others are not scandalized."

As to the distinction between initiation and vulgarization

the canonical template of Christianity at first little differed from those of the ancient Greek and Egyptian Sanctuaries.

The warnings were similar.

For example, the opening formulation used in the primitive Church, was:

---

[1] At Saint Cyril's time all the non-initiates in Celestial sciences were named "gentile". Gent is equivalent to Hebrew "goy", designating a being rooted in and related to Earth only.

"Profanes, get away! Let the non-initiate Catechumens depart."

In the same way at Eleusis, the sacred herald was proclaiming to the crowd:

"Ekas, ekas este, bebeloi! "

"Afar, Afar. o ye the profanes."

Likewise, in polytheistic Rome, the sacerdotal heralds of the ancient Etruscan rite shouted, before closing the sacred doors of the Temples on the Initiates:

"Procul, o procul este, profani! "

"Keep away, keep away, profane ones!"

"Let the non-initiate leave."

Similar to the Greek and Roman template was the profound distinction established by Jesus between the Intelligible Mysteries contained in his Testamentary Doctrine and the evangelical Morality, later preached by the primitive Church.

The part of Jesus' revelation which pertains specifically to 3 Fundamental Essences constitutive of the" Father's Divine Kingdom", was intended to be disclosed as 3 degrees of knowledge reserved to Sacerdotal Initiates.

Nonetheless. the originators of the primitive Church chose to divulge those 3 degrees of knowledge by presenting them to the faithful as 3 symbolic "personae", so establishing the Divine Ternary of the traditional Christian creed. (Father-Son-Holy Spirit).

For the Faithful

the Catechization and the access to the sacraments constituted the Purification and moral Preparation.

Initiation to the Mysteries was allowing the initiate to reach the Perfection specifically intended by Jesus and his disciples, which they designate as:

"Advent of the Kingdom",

"Worship in Spirit and Truth",

"Paraclete" and " Promise".

Thus, on the outside, so to speak, in the exoteric Cult, the person of the Son was the supreme representation of the Apotheosis of the Great Christian Hierophant, while the Gospel represented his call to the moral preparation of the human species.

On the inside, esoterically, behind the altar of Christ, the Mysteries of the Father and of the Holy Spirit safeguarded the secret religion of Jesus, its principles, the true aims of his revelatory proclamations as well as the necessary moral preparation, the sciences, the applied arts, the scientific methods required to realize the fulfillment of the Promise and achieve supreme revelation of Perfection.

Thus, through high Initiation,

the individual could be reintegrated into the superior Regnum of the Species; then, finally, in the course of time, the Divine Kingdom, thanks to the efforts of human Perfectibility, could be established in the terrestrial social organism as it is in the Heavens.

The lively enthusiasm with which St. Clement of Alexandria speaks of the safeguarded Mysteries demonstrates they were not purely nominal, certainly not fictional:

"O sacred Mystery of Truth."

"O immaculate Light."

"Illumed by the light of the torches, the skies reopen, and the Divinity is being revealed!"

"Here I am, I have become Saint: I am an Initiate!"

"Here is the Lord, the Hierophant.
He affixes his seal on the adepts, after having illuminated them with Its rays; and to reward their Faith, the Lord Hierophant will reopen the gates of the Father's Kingdom!

"Come and share the sacred Sciences, celebrations of my Mysteries: come and ask for Initiation!"

Jesus, by thus dividing his teaching

in two categories, if not in three, one devoted to external propagation, to the quick and widespread diffusion within the masses;

the other teaching, safeguarded, accessible only to a selected few, is a true Higher Initiation which, through the march of events and the passing of time, enables the creating of a movement able to organize already evangelized societies.

Moreover, Jesus, in this as in everything, was in line with the Truth inherent to all the Higher Initiations and with the wisdom of all ancient Initiators.

Thus does Moses operate, assigning to oral tradition and through a specially constituted corps of Initiates, the keys to decipher his written word revealing and clarifying the Mysteries of the Father.

Thus operates Orpheus[1]; and ***thus Pythagoras*** also separates his teaching in two categories, on one side Purification, on the

---

[1] Orpheus and Moses were contemporary, both High Initiates in the Temple of Thebes, Egypt.

other Perfection, respectively named Katharsis[1] and Teleiates[2].

Therefore, behind all the altars of the ancient civilizing societies, the external cult safeguarded the Higher Religion.

Religion then being the integral Truth, expressed in Greece as a triple hierarchy, expressed in Egypt as a quadruple hierarchy of Sciences, their corresponding applied Arts and their canons.

So much so that this fully comprehensive view of Perfection,

this Synthesis of encompassing Sciences, these precise keys opening the knowledge of the Grand Art and Life, were so carefully shielded from the profane world so as to remain protected from ignorance, the tyranny of the vulgar, and the anarchy of opinions.

Such is the secret of the strong constitution of society, family, individual

---

[1] Katharsis: Arts pertaining to purification and purgation of emotions and passions.

[2] Teleiates: Arts enabling attainment of perfection.

characters within the Greek and Roman republics, and within the sacerdotal sovereignties which preceded them.

Following the dereliction and discredit of the Mysteries, ensued social anarchy, civil discord, a tyrannical control annihilating the ancient freedoms.

In the past, for centuries, in Christendom

the Mysteries so clearly revealed in St. Cyril's writings have become somewhat obfuscated.

Today, while minimally preserved in the form of sacraments, they have become, in the mind of the secular society, entirely fictitious.

In our times,

the Spirit of the Promise requires from us that we focus on the task of perfecting the present condition, not on criticizing it; therefore, sidestepping the study of the causes of this sad reality, let us examine their gravest consequences.

The Sciences, the applied Arts, Nature, Life, are henceforth abandoned to the profane world, and, in that regard, this world is lacking religious and spiritual recourse, either against its own profanations, or its own ignorance, or its own unconsciousness.

Understandably, this religious and spiritual dimness might be an unavoidable cyclical occurrence; but that this dimness must perdure, one cannot answer affirmatively after a serious examination of this issue so important to harmonious social evolution.

After having slowly freed themselves, through naturalistic modern sciences, from the rigid tutelage of the Church, nearly all the inherent faculties human perfectibility may possess are nowadays armed with most of their means of intellectual action;

although their fundamental Principles, their abilities for combining and synthesizing, are wanting, as well are wanting the various methods which can recognize and define the laws regulating the hierarchical relations of these Principles and abilities.

Claimed in the name of Nature,

this new intellectual liberty opposes Nature to God and Cults, and, in politics as well as in sociology, it leads to an anti-religious, indefinite movement towards a socially indeterminate goal.

This claimed freedom encircles the Churches and their correlated social order, thus isolating them from the general stream of ideas and facts.

Evoking the miracles of industry, this newly found freedom enthralls and fascinates the minds, agitates the mirage of luxury and the lyricism about natural matter; it also induces humankind to re-capture all its rights, often at the cost of its duties; it deploys the fairytale of a wondrous civilization only to feed instinctual appetites;

furthermore, it generates in the Christian world a general tremor which tends to destroy its religious and social foundations, while it does not seem qualified to replace them.

Here is the list of oppositions

which a renewed Theology and contemporary Christianity must confront:

-I- *Opposition to Genesis.*

To the Septuagint Version in the Greek Church, to Saint Jerome's Version in the Latin Church, to the Translations of these translations into many national languages, *the Naturalistic[1] mind opposes a counter-Genesis*, starting from the first two words (everything arises solely from natural causes) which involve the negation

---

[1] Naturalism: the viewpoint according to which **everything arises solely from natural properties and causes**, and supernatural or spiritual explanations are excluded or discounted.

of the rest (supernatural and spiritual causes).

So, to the Theological Genesis the Naturalism opposes an Anti-Genesis[1].

-II- *Opposition to the Decalogue* *(Moses' Ten Commandments),*

Moses had attached the Divine Law to Moral Rules and Duties, so conjoining Moral Duties to corresponding Rights.

Breaking that bond,

Naturalism opposes to Moses' Decalogue, under various designations:

Human rights,

Natural rights,

Free conscience,

Independent Morale,

therefore creating a *Counter Decalogue, or Anti-Decalogue.*

---

[1] Anti-Genesis= elimination of any reference to Divinity in the recital of Creation of the Universe, the apparition of Life and its evolution.

-III- *Opposition to Theology,* (Science of the invisible Structure of the Grand Universe)

not only to Christian theology, but also to Talmudic and Koranic Theologies,

Naturalism, denying all divine action in the social state, and every divine science,

brashly opposes against Theology the Creed of

A-theology   (Anti-Theology)

-IV- *Opposition to Christ's PROMISE*

the great organic treasure of Christianity, (and through it of Israel and Islam) which, supported by the Sepher Boehreshith (Genesis), and on behalf of the Principles contained therein, can promulgate the Heavenly and earthly aims of Organic Societies, the perfect goal of Perfectibility,

Naturalism suppressing Perfection, past and future, as to its aims and Principles,

opposes a Counter Promise:
an Indefinite Progress, that is,
an Anti-Promise.

Each of these four divisions embraces, in its synthesis, a whole hierarchy of degrees by which, in the name of ***experimental Naturalism,*** Anti-Genesis is opposed to Genesis, Anti-Decalogue to the Decalogue, A-Theology to Theology, Anti-Promise to the Promise.

I prepared tables (not yet published as of 1877), which, afterwards and if necessary, will allow, just as clearly, to anticipate the political and social, civil, and familial oppositions engendered by these theological and rational antagonisms[1], within the State, Society, City and Home.

Thus, in Christendom,

human Minds are opposed into two camps, on which this double doctrine

---

[1] At the time of this translation (2019-2020 AD) those antagonisms and their multiple effects are easily perceptible.

hangs like the divided gods over the Greek and Trojan heroes.

Political and social facts bear and will increasingly bear the imprint of, suffer and will suffer more and more the effects of this ideological battle, a real civil war of the minds, leading to the anarchy within peoples and human affairs, as well as the reign of force at the helm of societies.

I have long believed that this war was ineluctable, at that time I was not able to conceive clearly the possibility of bringing a long-lasting organic peace.

After long research and longer meditations, I am now convinced that a lasting peace is possible.

In this chapter, I previously evidenced that within the Primitive Church Christianity has kept in reserve a whole set of knowledge, doctrines and programs known as Mysteries;

it remains to show how Christianity can now accept the truths uncovered by Natural sciences and recognize the many legitimate demands for freedom and truth claimed by individuals and societies.

And Christianity should not only conform superficially to the novel ideas of Progress already pervading contemporary Christendom;

it must also, by profound and specific contributions, participate to the completeness and realization of that Progress, so as that True Progress will be exceeding the cherished fantasies and confused expectations based exclusively on the paradigms of naturalism.

Yes or no?

Is Judeo-Christianity, by its texts, the letter and the spirit of the first two Testaments, empowered to recognize Nature as a Puissance?

Is it empowered to discern Nature's Rights and Merits in the Universe and consequently in the Social State?

Is not Judeo-Christianity genuinely qualified to validate, even enhance, that which, in Science, Applied Art and Human Living Experience, emanates from Nature? Knowing that Nature itself clearly bears the seal of the Divine Authority imprinted upon all Organic Substances of beings and things?

The answer is Yes.

Regarding the *question of Love and Sexes*, beyond ordinary exoteric Theology, it is in the Heights of "Theogony", from the base to the summit of the Mysteries of the Father, that the key to this fundamental problem must be sought.

From Moses' legacy, Christendom, Israel, Islam, can and must extract the exact key opening our world to the messianic promise: *a higher spiritual state and a perfected social organism.*

For it is in the hieroglyphic encrypted message of the Hebrew text of Moses' Cosmogony that are sealed, at three levels, the Mysteries of the Father, which the Primitive Church taught only to the future Initiates to the Great Mysteries, and which Jesus safeguarded for the time when Revelation is fully accomplished.

At first glance, when opening Moses' text in Hebrew, and even when one adds to it the messages of Tradition, it seems the author of the Sepher Bœreshith has kept in the fog the Theogonic [1]question of the Sexes.

His admirable Cosmogony in Hebrew, entirely different from the vulgar translations, justifies at every word its title of Cosmogony, by revealing an absolute Science of the Principles operating in the Universe and at work in the social state; though, regarding the Essence of Divinity itself, Moses' text appears lacking any Theogonic light.

---

[1] **Theogony:** science describing the origins, genealogies, and hierarchies within the Divine kingdom. To our knowledge the URANTIA BOOK is the only modern work offering an in-depth THEOGONIC study

Hence the Sexes remain unexplained as to their Principle.

They are poorly defined as to their Finality, forever opposed, fated in Religion as in Society either to mutual scolding, or to reciprocal claim of freedom worse than enslavement itself.

Theogony only could solve this predicament, as the latter holds a prevalent position in the organic Constitution of the Universe as much as in that of the Social-State; but unfortunately, Christianity, Israel, Islam, have at the base of their respective orthodoxies, only a Cosmogony[1]; they do not have a Theogony.

Moses' original teaching included the *ontological Principles and Faculties of the Divinity*, thus not solely revealing the divine

---

[1] Modern 21rst Century "cosmogony" is in fact exclusively a "cosmology", describing only the materialistic aspects of the "Universe". Real "cosmogony" would reveal the meta-physical and hyper-natural aspects of the Universe. Modern Quantum physics is an attempt to reignite the quest for true cosmogony, through a multidimensional scientific synthesis aiming at re-acquiring the secretive cosmogony of all religious creeds.

generative actions throughout the Universe. That ontological science initially formed the first 9 chapters, while the current legacy of Moses, begins only at the 10th chapter; that is, the Cosmogony, starting with the famous word *Bœreshith* ("In the Beginning").

Question: Why Moses, High Initiate of the Egyptian temple of Thebes, who was to become the Initiator of the Hebrews, did suppress the first 9 chapters (in his Genesis Book) which conveyed the Science of the first and highest degree in the hierarchy of divine knowledge?[1]

An in-depth meditation on the history of the ancient Cults, States, societies of Asia and the Mediterranean coast, starting at the time of the Schism of Irshou

---

[1] The authentic Kabala refers to those 9 absent chapters as *A-tzilut* , the knowledge of true Theogony (science of Divine Essences), symbolized by the letter *A-leph.* The current book of Genesis starting with the letter B *(Bereshit*) reveals only the three lower degrees of divine Theogony-science of Existences/Substances): *Beriah* (Creation-manifestation*), Yetsirah* (design-intent*), Aassiyah* (actions and conscience).

(circa 5,000 BC) shows that Moses' decision was motivated and justified by his profound wisdom.

There are times in the history of societies when light must give way to some measure of obscurity, lest the darkness extinguishes entirely all the light.

Today, the general circumstances in Europe are far from what they were then in Asia.

Natural sciences are now so widespread, lifestyles have moved so much forward, that the religions and their inherent social order, cannot any longer, without endangering their very existence, limit themselves either to recrimination, resistance or to intellectual stagnation.

Western civilization, hurtling at full speed in the path of industrial progress, needs a spiritual and religious enlightenment all the more precise, needs an integral revelation all the more perfect, that all the faculties of perfectibility are overstimulated, despite the fact that their light comes from below and not from above.

It is up to the Creeds which have in common the powerful memories of the Mysteries of the Father, to accept or reject the facts, the ones I just presented to the reader and the ones I am about to present.

The only Theogonic elements of divine science included within Cosmogony and which is common to the three main religions, are encrypted within the specific Names used by Moses, whenever he is evoking Divinity.

He does so either to directly reveal the Divine Essence or to describe particular aspects of the divinely created Universe.

These names are mainly *Jehovah* and *Elohim*, real nominal hierograms, which must be decrypted with the proper keys.

"Elohim" represents the operative Puissances efferent from the Sovereign Divinity of our Universe and acting within Humankind's Social State;

"*Jehovah*" represents the Sovereign, Central Constitution of these operative Puissances.

"Elohim" therefore pertains to Cosmogony, while Jehovah pertains to Theogony.

Therefore, while seeking within these sacred Names the key to the *question of the Sexes-Genders* and the Mystery of the Father Creator, I will focus my study only *on the hierogram "Jehovah".*

In order to insure this important theogonic mystery is properly elucidated, I will call on the keeper of the Mysteries of the Father and of Moses' Oral Tradition: the High Priest of the ancient Temple of Israel; he will himself reveal the hidden meaning of this famous tetragrammaton: יהוה in Hebrew and **YHWH** in Latin script.

Thus, his answer will come to us from the depth of past centuries.

Indeed, once a year, in the sanctuary, at a ritually well-defined time, facing the assembled priests, the High Priest opened the Tetragrammaton, and revealed the Divine "Schema", that was to be listened and heard.

So he was enouncing: יהו
Iod-Hé-Vav-Hé! Y H W H

The assembled priests were answering:

Shem-Hamme-Phorash[1]

The High Priest then was adding:

Iod-Hevah! (Ioud Chavah)

and on this point, I call to attention the savants of the three major religions, because, thus re-assembled, the letters of the Tetragrammaton meant: **Masculine-Feminine.** (unbreakable union of)

And the priests were repeating in chorus:

Shem-Ha-Me Phorash שם המפורש

Meaning: "The name is accurately pronounced!".

---

[1] *Shem*=the Name-Absolute Vibration, *Hamme*=spirit activator (Ham) of matrix of Life (Me), *Phorash*=Ignating (Phor), radiating. (Rash).

It is in this sense that Jesus Christ said: *"Let Your Name be sanctified!"*

Orpheus, initiated in the same Egyptian sanctuaries as Moses, has included the following declaration in one of his rituals: *"Zeus is, at once, the Divine Bridegroom and the Perfect Bride."*

From what precedes, it follows that Moses did not construe the unity of God the Father as an abstraction, but as the absolute, infinite union of the two generating Puissances that constitute Him, Father of beings *and* Creator of things.

Let us give these two powers the names that correspond to them in our languages:

Eternal-Masculine | Eternal Feminine.

God | Nature.

Essence | Substance.

The name Elohim,

commonly translated, *He-She*[1]*-the-Gods,* encompasses the whole hierarchy of the Principles, of the Causes, of the Organic *Forces that God unfolds in Nature,* and that Nature folds back in God;

so is expressed the total communion, the perfect union of their Essence, their Substance, from which the Universe is the resulting effect.

For ultimate comprehension, Ultimum Organum, two important inferences emerge from this Mystery of the Father, from that Theogonic secret learned from the Egyptian sanctuaries by Moses and Orpheus and of which Jesus Christ, in his prayer[2], indicates the great import.

The first inference concerns the genealogical *tree of Science*; the second, the genealogical *tree of Life.*

---

[1] He-She= reflecting the unbreakable Union of the Masculine & Feminine Principles.
[2] On the Mount of Transfiguration (Luke 9:28-29)

With regard to Science[1], and thanks to this inferred savant knowledge (Union of Opposite Complementary), the churches, the synagogues and the mosques, restoring the Initiation to the Mysteries of the Father, will be able to reduce gradually among the educated people, the present antagonism of Genesis versus Anti-Genesis, Promise versus Anti-Promise, Theology versus Atheology, Decalogue versus Anti Decalogue.

The sacerdotal Christian bodies, represented by their bishops, when congregating and collaborating with the lay savants of the universities, will offer them a religious consecration; they will then agree together on the need for an "Ultimum Organum", instrument of precision indispensable for establishing a true hierarchy within the Natural Sciences and their corresponding applied Arts:

_____

[1] The Principle of Opposite Complementarity is the founding unifying law of Quantum Physics (see Niels Bohr – major founder of Quantum Mechanics).

First, they will clearly define the appropriate methodologies for the natural sciences, **secondly** the specific methods pertaining to human sciences and, **thirdly**, the methodology suitable for studying the Divine Hierarchy.

Finally, they will reveal the correlation linking these three sets of Laws with the Cosmogonic Principles, such as they are encrypted within the name of the Father, by Moses, in the Hebrew text of *Sepher Bœreshith (Genesis).*

All this may occur because the knowledge of the *Mysteries of the Father* and the *Mysteries of the Holy Spirit* have been carefully safeguarded by the initiates of the Christian, Israelite and Muslim sacerdotal bodies.

To religious men and women, I say:

Be daring, have no fear!

Push the limits of the human mind: the result will infinitely increase, in the Social State, the majesty of Divinity, the dignity of humankind and your own authority.

Contrary to common contemporary opinion, Moses, Jesus Christ, both have given you all the necessary resources to develop human perfectibility up to divine perfection.

There has occurred a temporary abandonment of the Ancient Sciences[1] and their applied Arts, as well as the abandonment of the study of Life, to the sole secular savants, due to the obfuscation and the quasi disappearance of the initiatic Mysteries of the Father and the Mysteries of the Holy-Spirit.

This has left the intellectual faculties guideless as to the present, aimless in regard with the future, devoid of fundamental principles, thus engendering the methodological confusion, the antagonism of doctrines which are now bewildering Christendom.

---

[1] The author expands on that Ancient Sciences in his book "Mission of the Jews" and "The Golden Thread of World History).

However, these evils are not without remedy,

and to heal them, everything has been given to you in the past, everything will be given to you now and in the future.

One need not fear to resolutely tackle this ideological antagonism, this methodological confusion.

The anarchy of the sciences has its remedy in Science itself,

for Integral Science[1] *is inseparable from Integral Truth.*

Let's understand that *complete Integral Science,* comprises four hierarchies of sciences,[2] each one unfolding truth through its own specific methods.

---

[1] Integral means integration of Natural Sciences with Divine Sciences. Note that the irruption of Quantum Physics reveals laws apparently antagonistic with purely naturalistic classical science. Therefore, advanced science is experimenting with laws pertaining to the hyperphysical aspects of the Universe, so far contained in the Divine Sciences and creeds.

[2] Divinity / Cosmos / Humankind /Nature.

All four hierarchies will be validating their findings in their splendid wholeness, granting a magnificent support to each other.

They will, in the future, in the name of the Mysteries of the Father and of the Holy Spirit, be yet again conveyed through graduated Initiations (each specific to Sex identity, ages, degree of consciousness).

These re-established Initiations will occur as well in Churches, Universities, States, Homes, in accordance with the vow and *promise of Jesus Christ to bring about on Earth the order ruling the Kingdom of Heaven.*

This order, in the Heavens, reigns by the medium of Pure Light, while in the social state on Earth, it uses Knowledge and Consciousness as Organic Light.

The restoration, by the savant sacerdotal bodies, of the quadruple hierarchy of Sciences which constitutes Integral

Knowledge, is a task far less difficult than it is believed to be.

The great work, although incomplete and devoid of any religious foundation, effected on natural sciences by Francis Bacon, based solely on direct analysis, sensory experience, and sensory observation, is enough to demonstrate that, one can as well restore, with the same precision, the *Integral Science*.

If the intellect of a sole individual has impressed upon Europe the formidable scientific impulse which is still powering it today, imagine what could be accomplished in favor of Integral Science and Complete Truth, if Christian bishops, as a wholly integrated group, were willing to meet and work with the highest secular thinkers, the most intelligent and best-informed minds among all the savant bodies of their time.

Let us assert, once again, that the experiential learning methods and specific knowledge encompassed by the ancient

Mysteries[1], as indicated by St. Cyril and St. Clement of Alexandria, offer a prospective framework, a tested predetermined form in which this intellectual movement can take place.

The graduated Initiations, each specific to Sex, Age and level of personal Consciousness, provided in the past by the primitive Church, may now be reinstated and reopened to all people of high intelligence and strong good will.

Finally, due to the commendable configuration of the educational institutions based on the Christian ternary symbolism (Father-Son-Holy Spirit), nothing in the actual teaching of the Churches, strictly directed to mass education, would

---

[1]Mysteries of Father and Holy Spirit, similar to ancient Egyptian Initiations, are qualitative scientific approaches to Theogony (Divinity and Deities), to Cosmogony (Study of the Living Universe and sub-universes) as yet unexplored by naturalistic science of Cosmology. Also, as yet unexplored is the Nature of Humankind (beyond physiology, biology) including experimental study of spiritual realms and Souls.

involve any structural changes disturbing the faithful.

Thus, the cult of the Son would provide again what it has been providing at the time of the primitive Church: the moral purification of each Initiate.

It would not be only what it has become since the initiatic Mysteries have been interrupted and gone into oblivion: namely *a mere general call to some vague salvation.*

Therefore, it is at the very center of the religions and at the heart of their reinstated initiatic Mysteries that Principles, aims and ways to effect their eventuation, would be revealed to the deserving ones as Science, applied Arts and essence of Life; for such was the teaching at the time of the primitive Church, and long before[1].

Thus, the genealogical Tree of Science, once restored to its sacred ground, can

---

[1] Among the sciences initially taught was Psychurgy, a means of contact with and action on visible and invisible realities, often called "Miracle".

breathe above the profane world, and ceasing to be desecrated, will expand its roots into the promised land, deploy and plunge its branches into all the luminous altitudes of the Truth.

Thus, every scientific fruit of this Symbolic Tree, instead of being devoured by all without discernment and without method, can be re-attached to its original branch, to its hierarchical degree, clearly showing its position within the whole.

Thus, every scientific fruit will penetrate the human understanding only through the eyes of highly enlightened intelligence, through the applied art corresponding to each science, through the intellectual faculty corresponding to each application.

Thus, finally, in the whole of Christendom, in every State, in every home, will progressively fade away the ideological battle between spirit and matter manifesting into religious, social, and political conflicts; a war whose general causes are rooted in the seemingly irremediable antagonism of Genesis and anti-Genesis, the Decalogue and Anti-Decalogue, Theology and Atheology, Promise and the Anti-Promise.

This war, expanding into multicolored and multifaceted battles, divides Christianity, besieges Christianism, stifling it, and preventing it from harmoniously functioning, in concert with Israel and Islam (with regard to the principles and aims they have in common).

That war bars, in Europe, Asia, Africa, the unfolding of the Great Masterwork of Christic Civilization, namely the full advancement of the human mind toward the Truth attached to the knowledge of all the Sacred Promises.

And thus, it prevents the reforming of the entire social state into the perfect organic constitution which Jesus the Christ calls the Kingdom of God, and of which he has predicted the advent on Earth.

Certainly, the regeneration of

the genealogical Tree of the Sciences within the religious teachings, leads to the revival of the Tree of Life at all levels of the Social-State.

The applied Arts Issued from those Divine Sciences, will re-acquire through Initiation, their aesthetic canons, their principles, their aims, their methods, and will easily restore to Life its heights, its sacred depths; to the genius mind it will restore its "raison d' être;" family and social relationships will regain their stability and dignity.

Individuals, families and societies, now safeguarded from the venality and banality of the diluted and solely economic civilization, wandering as exiled gods banned from their sanctuaries, they will be able to breathe the Divine Light above the profane world, and they will put an end to their self-inflicted deviation.

Once again, they will become what they have been in ancient Greece, namely the conscious manifestation of Perfect Beauty, the enchanting reflection of the Perfect Truth.

And among all the sacred High Arts, there is one which only the Mysteries of the Father and the Mysteries of the Holy Spirit can absolutely express in its Divine Beauty and Divine Truth, a gift to the human soul fervently calling for it.

This supreme Art, which corresponds to Ontology in the order of Sciences, corresponds to Motherhood in the order of the human Virtues.

This may give rise to the progressive full fledge renaissance of the *Eternal Feminine,* by the *re-establishment of the special Initiations* which the Greek women benefited from in Greece thanks to the all feminine sanctuaries which Orpheus had established for them, and which, perhaps, women in the primitive Christian Church were still members of; for, we know that, for a time, in Egypt and Ethiopia, women had their own priesthood.

The Mystery of the Father's Name - IEVE- allows for a dyadic Initiation, one reserved for the *Eternal Masculine*, the other for the *Eternal Feminine*.

In this Mystery of the Father's Name, one can discern that if the *Male Principle* exercises its authority and unfolds its cosmogonic forces upon *the Essence of Beings*, the *Feminine Principle* in the universe unfolds its authority and reveals its powers through the organic *Substance of Beings*.

The Essence of Beings is co-existential with **I** (=Iod), which conveys the Masculine Principle, first term of the complete name **I E V E** (Iod-He-Vav-He);

but the existence and sustenance of the Beings, their transformation and their preservation belong to **E V E** (=He-Vav-He), Feminine PRINCIPLE (whom we call Creative Nature), true Spouse of the Father.

The *Love that unites them forever* has been recognized by all the ancient cosmogonies as the Principle and the Goal of their *indissoluble Unity*.

Sanchoniaton, Moses, Orpheus agree on this point as on many others.

Creative Nature, united to God by the power, the mutual bond of Love, engenders everything out of nothing.

Without this supreme bond, which constitutes the foundation of the Union of the Sexes and Marriage, this engenderment which creates and builds the Universe would collapse entirely.

In the Christian ternary, the divine Spirit, the Holy Spirit, is Love itself; It is the breath of Life, concerning the psychurgical or vital animation of the Beings; it is Truth and Wisdom, regarding their intellectual animation, their spiritual resurrection, in humankind as well as in the hierarchies of beings which connect humankind to Divinity.

The real name "Love-Holy Spirit" is present in the Cosmogony common to the three major religions.

In the mind of Moses, the Holy Spirit is not a mere abstraction (the Egyptian priests, his masters, never wasted their time in metaphysical reveries), but the Holy Spirit is *a real Power* within the hierarchy of divine Powers.

Moses, High Initiate from the temple of Isis and Osiris, names this Puissance *Rouah Elohim*, meaning the breath of *Him-Her*-The-Gods.

(When studying the hierarchy of cosmogonic forces according to the method of the Divine Sciences, one finds this Puissance positioned no farther from Integral Light than the quarter of a diatonic, preceding and creating that Light within any state of chaos, whatever the state of these chaos).

The Feminine is to the Masculine,

in the social state, what Creative Nature is to God in the Universe, what a

Virtue is to a Principle at any level in the hierarchy of operativities, like duration is to time, like expanse to space, shape to concept, like brightness to the day, heat to fire, and Earth to Heaven.

But for the reciprocal to be true, Man must be for the Woman the real representative of God, the true reflection of His image.

Without enlightened religion, without initiatic teachings specific to each Sex, this condition cannot be fulfilled; and the bond, the strength that unites God and Creative Nature not finding in humankind sufficient intellectual and moral support, causes the marriages and homes, unions, and generations, to be left to chance, to unconsciousness, ignorance and resulting ontological weakness.

If Greece, as constituted by Egyptian High Priest Orpheus, has produced by thousands powerful geniuses and beautiful characters, one may not attribute that brilliance to the Mediterranean climate, but rather to the strength of conjugal bonds, to the Science and the High Art of Motherhood.

Montesquieu judiciously observed that the celebrated virtue of Greek wives was as proverbial as their feminine grace and their maternal science and art.

However, he only perceived one single source to that feminine grace and virtue.

Being particularly attentive to the spirit of the laws, he did not see *that the laws are almost always the average product of mores and faith*;

and, contrary to his views, Virtue, this moral power of the republics, is neither a fruit born only from political institutions, nor resulting solely from the phraseology of legislators or rhetoricians, philosophers or sophists.

If the maternal and feminine faculty has endowed Greece with such a pure and providential brilliance, if the successive generations have been so beautiful and powerful, it is to the *Orphic Feminine Initiations* and the organic constitution of the homes that the genuine origin of that brilliance is to be found.

I do not wish to lift fully the veil of these profound Life Mysteries, and I will confine myself to induce and invite others to make their own discoveries.

It will be enough for me to emphasize again this saying of Jesus, *Hallowed be your Name*, admirably concordant with the rituals of Orpheus and the theogonic secret encrypted by Moses in the static hieroglyph of the Divinity YeHVe/IEVE.

Today, in many European countries and elsewhere, *the feminine question, stirred from a civil and even political point of view*, is giving rise to a turmoil which may become detrimental to the peace of the Home, to the tranquility of the City, and even damaging to the real happiness of Women themselves.

City and State, civil and political concerns, have sadly for long been the prerogative of Men, and they might see it temporarily disputed, though, sooner or later they will seize it again by forcing their Rights on the ill inspired other Sex who grabbed the burden of duties from them.

But in the Home, Family, Civilization, in the Organic Economy of Life, the Woman, represented by "HeVeh / **EVE**" within the integral Name of the Father Ye-HeVeH /**I-EVE**, as Creative Nature in the Constitution of the Universe, is not half but *three quarters of the Male Principle.*

Generator and conservator of life, arts, civilization, guardian of the generations, being invested by Creative Nature to have power over substance, it is at this level of reality that Women, through specific Initiations, will find back all their rights while fulfilling all the duties which their Feminine Virtues entail, thus acting to their own benefit, to that of Men, and to that of the entire Social State.

Presently, in regard with the mineral, vegetal and animal reigns, said to be inferior to humankind, the natural sciences, as shown in their resulting precise classifications, already contemplate the Tree of Life with a respect akin to religious awe.

Vegetal essences and animal species are carefully studied, selected, cultivated and guided towards the perfection which their potential of evolutive perfectibility implies.

Certainly, the culture of human generations demands no less science or art.

The principles and purposes of unions and marriages, breeding, general education, home education, should be treated with at least as much intelligence as the coupling of horses or bulls, the rearing, breeding and training of foals.

Until now, however, in Christianity, Judaism and Islam, the Feminine Principle, abandoned to itself, experiences at random the fatality of the generations;

thus, the Maternal Power, submitted to its instincts only, and not guided by its plastic, psychurgic and intellectual inherent characters, is far from bearing the divine fruits that it would certainly generate if, through Science and the Art of Motherhood, Women would revive the Providential Light and the vital Consciousness of their Sacerdotal vocation.

It is in the Mysteries of the Father and the Mysteries of the Holy Spirit, it is in the *Initiation to these Mysteries* that the Ultimum Organum -Ultimate Method- can reveal the possibility of a complete development of the Tree of Science, thus allowing for a perfect thriving of the Tree of Life.

First let's consider this fundamental TRUTH:

The *Eternal Masculine Principle*, being forever *incited* by *She-Nature* to ever subdivide *Him-self*, so as to multiply,

and being as well persistently induced by *She-Nature* to bestow *Her* with the whole initial Force of Motion, so that *Her* own Form and Substance may achieve cosmogonic plenitude, it consequently occurs that *He-the-Eternal-Masculine* causes *Him-self* to *be conquered by She-the-Eternal Feminine.*

However, the *Union of those two Eternal Principles is indissoluble*[1], total, perfect, and

---

[1] The past social covenants endeavored to mirror this Eternal Superior Principle by making human unions (marriages) indissoluble. At the present time (2020 AD), the Principle of Individual Liberty is attempting to supersede the Principle of Indissoluble Union of complementary opposite identities.

what I am about to say regarding *Death* does not imply anything against the existence and strength of this Union.

Every potentiality encompassed within the *Eternal Masculine Principle* becomes manifest and active within the everchanging fluidic substance of the *Eternal Feminine Principle.*

High Initiate of the Egyptian Temples-University, savant Moses refers to these entwined Principles as "ELOHIM" (*a plural form in Hebrew*); and to define LIGHT, a Force emanating from their combined activity, he uses the terms ROUAH ELOHIM (and not Jehovah).

Moses designates as "IONAH" the metamorphic substance of the Divine Spouse once fecundated by the Spirit and being on the way to generate a new Solar World, described by the encrypted name "NOAH", in a specifically defined cosmogonic field, which Moses names "THE-BAH".

In this *"Thebah"*, *this well circumscribed cosmogonic sphere, same in every solar world*, Life, that is the existence of Beings and the

Substance of things, originates from "Ionâh", the *Feminine Principle*, symbolized as an amorous dove, (represented in the sacred emblem of the ancient Ionians);

then, *"Ionah the dove"* follows the reflective course of Light -designated as "Ararat"- by refining and elevating the igneous essence of spirits, souls and bodies.

In every finite solar system of the Universe, *Death is manifesting as the return of individual beings to the wholeness of being*, the return of individual things to the oneness of original substance, that is "Tohu-Vah-Bohu".

Death is the expression of a cosmogonic power pertaining to the Male God, in tensional *opposition with Ionah the Eternal Feminine*, wherever Darkness stands opposed to Light.

Moses, major initiator of Israel, Christianity and Islam, names this power of Darkness: "Horeb".

Orpheus, who, like Moses, has been initiated in the sanctuaries of Egypt, gives to Darkness the same name: "Erebos", and he encrypts within the sound "IO"(*e-yo*) the presence of the initial impulse to the generating power of the Universal Mother .

In the cosmogony of Orpheus, "Erebos" designates the location-source of the *destructive power of the Father*; while in Moses' teaching, Horeb depicts the motion of the Father's devouring force.

This location-source can be construed as the corporeal shadow of all beings, or as the cone of darkness that every planet trails behind itself in the skies.

Such is construed the valley of the shadow of Death, never reached by the light of the sun, and visited only by the moon and the stars.

Let us dare to say it:

Yes, the Father's power is destructive,

for the reason that He is Creator. Whenever appropriate, God is Good; sometimes God is Terrifying.

Almighty, *He* is always, not over Nature but through "Her "medium, always Omnipotent over the sons of Man, through Nature's medium and through Humankind's actions.

Only the Eternal Feminine Principle preserves the Universe,

defending it forever against the overwhelming embrace of the Eternal Masculine.

Open the grand-book of terrestrial hieroglyphics; observe the roaring males, who bear the physical mark of God the Father; they would devour the little ones, if Nature, their Providence, did not watch over the mother's heart, and did not arm her so-called weakness with a terrible force to fight tooth and nail in order to preserve her children's life

In the family, nucleus of the social state of Humankind, the masculine in the father weighs heavily on the male child;

the father, often, dampens the child's intellectual and moral developments, by compressing the variations of the nascent personality under his own fully formed mold, willing to bend the male child to his own law.

On the contrary, the woman, living personification of Nature, being as diverse as Nature is, stimulates the development of all the child's potentialities.

The ancient temples, the ancient social constitutions were more enlightened than our societies in regard with these initiatic Mysteries.

There was then no misunderstanding regarding the roles of sexes and generational status within the family home, no confusion of ranks within the social State. The gynaeceum was a refuge for the woman, while the woman was the child's refuge.

True, women had, within the feminine sanctuaries, full access to Science, applied Arts

and to the knowledge attached to their sacerdotal position;
furthermore, they were well educated in the practice of generational rituals, a

precise method of veneration of and connection with the ancestors.

When these rituals were profaned by the banality and skepticism of the "neutered" civilized people, blasphemed by the squabbles of the "neutered" philosophers, insufficiently safeguarded by the "neutered" priesthood, then, the family and the city collapsed;

the confusion in the roles of sexes, of ages and of ranks, shattered and wiped out the real foundations of society, engulfed all hierarchic organization;

now chance alone is regulating the entrance of generations into life; the muddled family hearths were deserted by the ancestors; thus, Death, the terrible male power of the Father of the Universe overwhelmed the brilliance of the ancient world, devouring entirely its religious, political, and civilizational structures.

When society is in a state of disarray, one must prepare its rebirth by safeguarding the memory of the ancestors, and by protecting women and children.

If therefore one does not want the little boy to be the victim of an excessive coercing male power, one must keep the child away from him until he reaches its tenth year, thus ensuring that, until then, the father intervenes infrequently and that the mother, as a natural "priestess-queen", reigns over the early upbringing.

That is why, churches, synagogues, mosques,

in the name of the Holy Spirit, must revive the Supreme Father's testament, revealing its true illuming power, *uncovering from under the vernacular translation of Genesis the genuine Cosmogony of Moses*, thus taking back the civilizing initiative by restoring the initiatic teaching[1];

they must give access to initiation first to the women, then to the various age-classes, then to all social ranks later, to all the races.

---

[1] When Death is approaching, one must revisit the past. This process is the same for a person, a society, a clan, a tribe, a nation, humanity, because every Death is always followed by a Rebirth.

If this is not done, and done properly, do fear the incoming of global social death: for the Heavenly Father is wrathful, and the alarmed ancestors, since long, are warning the successive generations that the coming devastation is near.

Death is a kiss of God, a caress of the Universal Father.

That is why, as mother of the human generations, the woman fears God more than she loves Him; like the lioness, she trembles for her cubs, and listens anxiously to the distant rustling of the invisible realm.

That is also why, Jesus the Son has come to reassure all mothers and offered them His Promise; and now it is more than time to let the Spirit of Truth run freely its course, if we wish for the intercession of providential divine power to fully operate within human affairs.

Then, stand up, all of you who wish that Christianity, Islam and Israel be revived in a splendid transfiguration!

The present unveiling of some of the mysteries of Death will *halt the profanation of the mysteries of Life, and surely Rebirth will ensue.*

The ancient priests of the Great Pyramid of Gizeh murmured to the right ear of the new Initiate:

"Osiris, the Eternal Masculine is the dark side of God".

One must choose between the fulfillment of the Son's Promise and the Father's Last Judgment, between Life and Death.

May individuals and societies bravely emulate the women and fear God!

This fear is indeed the beginning of Wisdom.

Thus, wherever darkness combats Light, Death, expression of the Father's cosmogonic power, at once is present and invisible, at once active and latent.

Whenever Death, Queen of Frights, is diving on a family, the ancestors are moved long before it strikes. Mostly during sleep, the ancestors cast prophetic images into the sensitive brain of women; and, men also, though often mostly neutral as regards spiritual life, at times may become deeply troubled by dreams. Sometimes ancestors make themselves visible.

Not only at night, even in daylight, an overwhelming sadness pervades the feelings, oppressing the lungs, stifling the throat, anguishing the hearts.

The pets themselves feel the approach of destruction; mournful dogs howl; many a people witnessed the deep emotion which stirs the ancestors, leading them to put into motion inanimate objects in the home they endeared.

No eye has ever seen Death per se; no one seems called to die now; and yet Death is always near.

When Death, Cosmogonic Puissancc of the Father,

wishes to manifest itself, and before this Puissance ignites the fatal causes of death, Nature is moved, the Eternal Feminine is stirred; IONAH, the fluidic cosmogonic substance of Life vibrates on Earth and in Heaven, and the souls of the dead hurry to warn the Livings and rush to the aid of those who are dying.

However, it is only for the profanes and the profaners that Death shows itself inexorable and deaf.

Conversely, the Initiate calls Death or rejects it, arms it or disarms it,

attracts it or fights it, unleashes it or hinders it.

But these Sciences must remain veiled and not be revealed except behind the altars of Initiation.

Yet, by the power of her love, the Woman, human reflection of Nature, has, at times, stirred that black veil, thus pushing Death away.

I witnessed once a desperate physician announcing to a mother, "Alas! it would take a miracle!".

The mother remained alone at the bed-side of her child and the miracle happened.

If you want to die, call Death.

If you want to keep it away from a loved one, pray with all the power of your soul.

But know that when someone must absolutely succumb, when the fatal hour has come, have courage!

Keep an eye on the one who is fading away: never, never was your devotion more necessary.

The physician, feeling his art vanquished, mistakenly departs too soon.

The therapy of agony must replace the treatment of the disease;

the Psychurgical cures applied by the ancient initiate therapists must supplant the physical remedies which have now become inadequate.

After the priest has administered his admirable sacraments and recited his formulas, he is leaving, though much remains to be done.

To the administered rituals aimed at pacifying the lingering physical passions, should be added a real attunement to spiritual sensitivity, and a precisely formulated invocation addressed to the assembled ancestors.

Priests and physicians, having to minister to the many, cannot stay long in each home; therefore, the spiritual ministration to the dying and the living as well, must be effected by those who received the initiations safeguarded by tradition.

Thus, mother or father, wife or husband, daughter or son, sister or brother, *once Initiated*, will be able to provide to whomever passes away all the help that the moment of death requires.

And after the last breath, when you have closed the eyes of the beloved one, do not presume the soul has vanished; do not abandon this corpse to the vigil of professional mercenaries, for, the spirit who inhabited this body is more than ever thirsting for your intelligence and is craving for your love.

Listen intensely, and may your heart resonate!

The soul of the beloved departed

embraces, in its desperate whirlwinds, those who piously watch over the deceased while applying the Psychurgical Science and Art.

Still full of thoughts, feelings, and sensations attached to the physical existence, even more suffering from having exited its effigy than from having suffered in it, this soul, if devoid of initiatic knowledge, feels cut from its physical ties and cannot find any alternate ones; the soul, frightened, shivering, ascending then falling, devoid of initiative or intent, this soul is engulfed again in agony and fright.

For, now, this soul is neither responsive to the call of the Heavenly Genii, nor to the Ancestors' exhortation.

Its hypernatural clairvoyance and deep understanding are hampered by the memory of all the physical apparatus, eyes, and ears, now obliterated.

Moreover, as this soul was living on Earth,

the more it has attached itself to instincts and passions of the flesh, the more it has forgotten the true Science, the Love and Consciousness of its Immortal Life, and the more it has become prisoner of its physical body, fastened to this corpse now on its path to decomposition and annihilation.

The state of desperation displayed by mentally ill peoples gives but only a slight representation of these post-mortem sufferings which can last for centuries.

During the funeral wake, incite and invoke the powers of Nature with all your might, pray to God, be aware of all the good you are doing for the deceased.

For this soul sees nothing but the night, hears nothing but silence, measures nothing but the unfathomable; this soul has but one thought, one feeling, one sensation: *a whirlwind of terror*.

Reason and morality, these two bonds with the human milieu here below, are broken to pieces within this newly detached soul.

Its existential self is experiencing the beginning of its *Second Death*, as yet being unable to find solace in it; its individuality is still seeking its own identity within dissociated viscera without being able to find it; its own personality, now alien to itself, frantically looks for its true self within this dead brain and inanimate heart, without being able to reach anything.

Hanging over the Horeb, this devouring abyss created by the absolute absence of sunlight, shivering, bewildered, without lungs to scream, without arms to wave, without eyes to see and cry, this soul aspires with all its strength to be reunited with that corpse which, (save for lugubrious exceptions), will remain as closed to it as the tomb will be.

For now this soul can only wander in utter horror.

The adept at Psychurgy, watching over the deceased, must endeavor to attract its attention.

If this adept succeeds, then, stirred, the soul starts exploring the darkness of its own blindness, the silence of its own deafness.

What is this soul searching for? As of yet it does not know: maybe a sign, a point of support, a light, a voice surging out of the turmoil.

The friend nearby this deathbed, being a learned psychurgue, all suffused with living vibrations, attracts the soul gradually toward his own beating heart, making it a radiant home, a sacred haven.

Vacillating, the soul approaches slowly and takes refuge near that welcoming heart, thus feeling elated and relieved.

Within that clairvoyant and warm flow of mutual empathy, the soul now draws courage, strength, spiritual potency.

This soul finally can pause,

accustoming itself to its new situation, it begins to perceive with a finer deeper sight, it understands with a mind not tainted by the physical senses.

It can gradually break the rational and moral ties imposed by its past emotions, passions and instincts; it can now distinctly perceive the Intelligible World, expand its innumerable spiritual potentials numbed since its birth in a material body;

therefore, it is *reconnecting with its inherent Ontological Principle, regaining possession of its Genuine Will.*

Like a migrating bird resting before starting a new leg on its long journey, this spirit has recognized its true identity, feeling to be now ready to confront the Horeb's abysses, and find there its direction.

As this Soul perceives other Souls,

notices the presence of the ancestors and of the winged Angel inviting it to soar, it briefly turns back toward the loving friend which held it, caressed it soulfully, a friend still praying and crying on the other side of Life.

Intensely and slowly, the departed, in turn, casts a loving breeze towards this pious and forlorn beating heart, filling it with an ethereal warmth, caressing it with an enchanting radiance, enfolding it with an exquisite spiritual embrace.

Then the escaping Spirit, speaking in the *ineffable Divine Language of Souls and Angels*, says:

" Thank you! Adieu! To God in Whom we shall meet again!"

ABOUT THE TRANSLATORS-AUTHORS
Contact E-mail: **archangel7997@gmail.com**

SIMHA SERAYA, is a Graduate of Paris Sorbonne University, major in Psychology and Sociology. Fluent in English, French, Hebrew and Classical Arabic, she is also a long-time dedicated researcher and discoverer of the fundamental linguistic components and elements constitutive of all languages, ancient and modern.

Author with Albert Haldane: **Angel Signs** *(2002)* **The Sacred Ten** *(2011) Mose's Ten Commandments Decrypted*

ALBERT HALDANE is a published poet author and philosopher. Continuing his classical education in ancient Greek and Latin, he graduated at Paris Sorbonne University, Master in Hellenistic and Renaissance Philosophy.

Translator of Saint-Yves d'Alveydre with Simha Seraya: **Mission of the Jews** 2020. **The Golden Thread of World History (2020) Initiation to the Mysteries of Birth Sexes & Love Death(2021)**